It's All About
Love

TO

KADM

ALL THE
Best

25 APRIL 2011

It's All About
Love

By
Leonard Weather Jr., M.D.

Tikur Press, Inc

Shreveport, Louisiana

Tikur Press, Inc.

2120 Bert Kouns Loop

Shreveport, LA 71118

ISBN 978-0-615-27152-1

Book design by Illumination Graphics

Printed by

Signature Book Printing, www.sbpbooks.com

To my mother Lucille Reese Weather,
her loving husband, Leonard Weather Sr.
and their children.
To your mother and father, their children
and all of the rest in the universe.

~ Epigraph ~

Throughout the ages love has been defined by countless people and in numerous ways. Love is the sum total of all of these, dispersed with truth, righteousness, peace, hope, joy and compassion. Love is you and He who created you.

Leonard Weather Jr., M.D.

Contents

CHAPTER SEVEN: ETERNAL LOVE

I

Love

I Love You Today

Today is Valentine's Day and
I love you, more than words
Can say. Tomorrow, will be
Another day and I will love
You the same as I did on
Valentine's Day.

My love for you is present
When the sun rises and when
It declines. It is present when
Stars sparkle high in the sky
And when the sparkle fades
Away. My love for you is
Present when it rains, snows
Even when it storms. It is
Present when the moon is
Full and when it can't be
Seen at all.

Darling my love for you is
Here to stay and is for the
Rest of time. I love you.

Happy Valentine's Day.

My Special Valentine

You are my special valentine,
My sweetheart, my queen, my
Earth angel, my pride and my
Joy. You are my precious one
Not just on the fourteenth of
February, but forever more.
Sweetheart, I can give you
Decorative boxes of candy
And flowers galore. I can
Give you heart shaped
Objects and items of love
From hundreds of stores.
I can give you diamonds
And pearls. I can send you
Singing telegrams, ribbons
And balloons of every color
For sure.
I will do all that can be done,
And more. For you are my
Special valentine and I'm
Yours forever and more...
I love you.

The Language of Love

I

  Love (English)
   Fekir (Amharic)
    maHabbi (Arabic)
     Lian ai (Chinese)
      Amour (French)
       Liebe (German)
        Amore (Italian)
         N ai (Japanese)
          Yonae (Korean)
           Amor (Portuguese)
            Amor (Spanish)
             Mapendo (Swahili)
              Karlek (Swedish)

         You.

No matter the language or
The land, I love you, just the same.

The Pursuit of Love

In the pursuit of love I
Looked in all the right
And wrong places. I
Gazed at many beautiful
Faces. I smiled, gave
Respect gave love, wined
And dined paid much
Received little, walked
And ran. I received
Many and researched
More. In different
Cities at various places.

I prayed much and was
Patient. I might have
Given up if it wasn't
For your call. I was
Caught by surprise,
If it wasn't out of love
Then it was out of
Kindness and a good
Heart. If it was the
Former it was fine and

If it was the latter it
Was even better, and
Greater. I felt good
And was elated. There
Was some hope, a sign?
You could be the one.
You are the one. My
Dream has come true.
The love of my life for
The rest of my days, a
True and genuine angel
Sent directly from heaven
Above.

It's Not Because

It's not because of your
Beauty or your great pride.

It's not because of your
Gentleness or kindness.

It's not because of your
Ingenuity or your
Personality.

It's not because of your
Vast intelligence or
Diligence.

It's not because of your
Lovely hair, face or skin.

It's not because of your
Stupendous family or
Unlimited love.

It's not because of you
But the love of God in
You.

I Do Love You

My love for you is
Greater than the sum
Of all the lakes, rivers
And seas in the universe
And more wonderful
Then all of these.
I love you even more
Than the beauty of the
Sun drifting above the
Glaring ocean as it sets
Beneath the tops of
Mountains and trades
Places with the moon.
Even until the Almighty
Takes us to His paradise
Above and until time
Stops and beyond that,
And more, I do love you.

Something

Something is happening
And I hope it won't end.
It's unique, intriguing,
Titillating; kind, gentle,
Loving and beautiful. It
Keeps me thinking,
Groping and seeking.

Something is understanding,
Loquacious and interesting,
Seems plain-attractive,
Extremely intelligent and
Copacetic. It's taking my
Time but not demanding
It's causing my heart to
Smile and my mind to be
Full of cheer.

Something is making me
Feel the comfort of a cool
Breeze during a hot muggy
August day.

It excites me so much
That I tremble with delight.
Something makes me want
To hold, caress and never
Let go and deserves the
Sweet love, kindness and
Togetherness that God's
Children should receive.

Something is physically
Comely, mentally strong
And a queen of the highest
Degree, shapely with proper
Curves, mature and yet
Youthful.

Something is beyond words
And the meaning that they
Denote. Something is
Obviously God sent...you.

I Can't See Love

I can't see air but
I feel it all around.

I can't see the wind
But I feel it touch
My skin.

I can't see sound
But I can hear it
With my ears.

I can't see time but
It goes on by.

I can't see your
Heart but I enjoy
The love that it
Imparts.

I can't see love
But I feel the
Warmth, joy and
Happiness that it
Presents.

II

More Love

Call on Me

Put your head on my
Shoulders and let me
Hold you in my arms.
Tell me your troubles,
So I can make the hurt
Dissipate. I can hug you
And comfort you until
You quiver with delight.
I am the maestro when
It comes to pleasing, the
One I love.

I can wipe away your
Tears and make you
Feel joyous, fill your
Life with wondrous
Cheer. I'm available
For you, for whatever
You need, then, now
And forever more.

Pleasing you is my
Mission and goal.
In time of need, no
Matter the extent

Of the discord, I can
Remedy it or know
Who can, call on me,
Please.

Right With You

I don't want to be
Wrong I confess.
I've been drawn
To you for a long
Time, and I love you.

If I didn't love you,
It would be wrong.
It would be like a
Cart pulling a horse
Or flowers growing
Soil. The sky shining
And not the stars. A
Full moon without
It's glow. It would
Be equivalent to a
Rainbow without
Colors, rain without
Drops or a fire with
Out a flame.

I don't want to be
Wrong I just want
To be right with you.

If

If, I were an ant, I would
Only stop working to
Look at you.

If, I were a leaf I wouldn't
Change colors in autumn
Unless, I got your
Permission.

If, I were a raindrop, I
Would not drop unless
I could wet your lips.

If, I were a star I would
Only shine when you
Looked at me.

If, I were a violent storm
I would only calm down
If you asked me to do it.

If, I were a singer I would
Sing to you night and day,
Just to see you smile.

If, I were a writer I would
Write you love letters, day
After day, after day.

Pure as Life

The full moon cast its beam
On mountains coated with
Snow and ice in the night.

The sun projects its mighty
Rays on the screen, the
Planet earth.

The summer wind fans
Beautiful flowers and trees
Spring rain, showers,
Vegetation and quenches
Thirst.

Ocean waves rise and fall
Except for structures of
Ice, stone and beaches of
Sand.

Birds chirp, children play
And butterflies waltz on
Air; bees seek pollen for
Sweet liquid gold.

Life is wonderful and my
Love for you is as natural
As nature, and as pure as
Life.

Recherche' is what I
Would say, darling I
Love you.

Joy

Joy is a cool summer
Night with the blatant
Glow of the moon, and
Stars communicating
Their presence via an
Array of twinkling
Codes.

Joy is the look in your
Eyes before our lips
Meet.

Joy is holding your hand
As we walk through the
Park.

Joy is cuddling up on a
Cold winter night in front
Of a radiant fireplace, with
Nothing else to do but to
Please you.

Joy is seeing you smile.

Joy is your smile.
Joy is what God defined
When He said we should
Be together forever and
The spirit of love would
Be its catalyst and seal.

The Song

I woke up this morning with a
Song and I almost called you
On the phone to sing it.

Oh, what a wonderful morning
The sun was shining and you
Were on my mind.

The summer flowers were
Swaying, spreading their
Fragrance as they moved
In harmony with the wind.

The ants were busy working
Building mounds and carrying
Objects as big as their bodies.

Spiders were busy spinning
Their webs in hopes of
Capturing a meal for the day.

Hummingbirds were darting
Back and forth from flower
To flower gathering royal
Essence for their subsistence.

Squirrels were playing and
Leaping from tree to tree.

Bees were collecting pollen
From colorful perennials
Laden with morning dew.

Everything was in motion,
Isn't life grand? By the way,
The song that I was going to
Sing, is called, "I love you,"
I love you.

III

Our Love

Thoughts and Dreams

I know the color of your attire
When you are a thousand miles
Away.

I can feel your touch, even when
You are not around. I can hear
Your footfalls in another town.

I can feel your lips even when
You are not kissing me. I can
Hear you speak when you are
A great distance away.

I realize an amazing sensation
When you think of me. I can
Hear your heart beat in the
Middle of a crowd.

I know your thoughts, I can
See your dreams.

I know what you want even
If you don't say.

Isn't love wonderful? That's
What you were thinking today.
Tonight, I will know your
Dreams.

Dream Come True

I had a dream the other
Night, that you and I
Was one?

We held each other and
Functioned as if our
Protoplasm were fused
Together.

Nothing could separate
Us from each other
Because God put us
Together.

We were together for
Ever and life was joyous
And fun.

I give many thanks and
Praises to the good Lord
Above for He made you
And my dreams come true.

Close to Me

I've been to many places, seen
Many faces, never have I seen
One like yours.

I have been to Africa, Asia,
Australia and Europe, never
Have I seen someone like you?

I've talked to many people
About thousands of subjects
But never to someone like
You.

I've won many hearts through
Struggles and battles but never
A heart that beats like yours.

I've walked with many people
Near and far but never the
Distance I walked with one
As comely as you.

I've kissed many lips through
The years but never as inviting
And wonderful as yours.
I've hugged and held many
But never as close to me as you.

Women Need Men

Some say "Waiting to Exhale,"
Teaches that women can do
Without men and don't
Need them.
On a cold wintry night most
Would say it's nice to be held
In the arms of a strong man
Or walk in the park on a warm
Spring day holding hands and
Let him steal a kiss when no
One else is present.
Who will fix the leak, the door?
Or that irritating drip? Then
There is the trash. What about
The outside lights? There's a
Lizard, a mouse and look a
Snake! What about the noise
Late at night? Is someone there?
Women need good men and
Men need good women.

Yours as One

I have one life to live just
With you. One pair of
Eyes to see the beauty of
You with. One pair of ears
To capture your heavenly
Voice. One pair of lips, to
Touch yours with. One
Mind to think of and
Heart to beat just for you.
One pair of arms to hold
You forever. One pair of
Legs to take me to wherever
You are. One body to be
Close to yours, one soul
Joined by the Almighty
To yours as one.

You Made Me Whole

I adore you and love you
Each second, minute and
Hour of the day. My love
For you has become
Greater and greater. It is
More powerful than words
Can express and even
Grows as I say these few
Words.

As seasons come and go
As years pass us by I can't
Deny that I need more
And more of your love.
Its insatiable, unlimited,
Uncomparable and
Unbelievable. You are
Better than the best and
Have made me forget
All the rest.

I never knew happiness
Until you came along. I
Never heard the words

Those robins sing and saw
Flowers play, trees wave
As birds fly away or the
Passionate fragrance that
Emanates from rubrium
Lilies or sterling silver
Roses until I fell in love
With you. You are my
Other half and loving
You have made me whole.

Feel the Love

You can feel the love
As she looks up at him
And smiles. Then it
Flows back as powerful
As a mighty hurricane
With the peace and joy
That only God could
Command, uniquely
Defined as
Miraculously Divine.

From the beginning
God made two
People who are one
For each other. When
You see her, you see
The goodness that is
He. When you see
Him you know that
The good of her
Is truly there. God
Did this it's all-good...
Love. That which is
More then pleasing

To the eye and spirit.
A love so pronounced
That when you see
Them you not only
See, you feel the
Love.

This is their story
Of the many years
Together and More
Forever.

Mae & Dr. Tracy

No Other Love Will Do

I don't know what you want
Out of life but I want you.
Hopefully, you want and need
Me as much as I need you.

I can make you feel better than
You ever felt, do things you've
Never been able to do, treat you
Better than you've ever been
Treated.

All that you ever wanted and need
Is yours for the asking. It's not to
Buy you off but simply to treat
You as the lady I love should be
Treated.

You can have me or reject me
That is, love me or leave me.
The choice is yours. Hopefully
The former, but whatever the
Choice nothing will ever erase the
Miraculous feeling that I have for
You. No other love will do, all
My love is reserved for you.

IV

Precious
Love

Power in the Word

Love is a wonderful feeling,
And is a state of life, like no
Other. It has incredible energy
And is more remarkable than
A shooting star. It has
Amazing power and strength
It proliferates, it grows and
Grows. Love never tatters and
Can wash away hurt. It can
Get rid of pain and can even
Heal the maimed.

Love is a universal language
And is understood by all
Without saying a word. It's for
The rich and the poor. It cost so
Little, you could say it's almost
Free. It's a four-letter word
With true power in the word.
It renders joy, it's true, real and
Everlasting.

Show Your Love

Men do not have to show
Their love by showering
Their lady with gifts, but
They should, even if it
Takes two occupations.

Providing a massage at the
Spa along with a pedicure
And manicure, is magnificent.

A surprise trip to Hawaii or
A Caribbean cruise is a real
Dream.

A glass of cold champagne
At the end of a miserable
Day is more than refreshing.

Two dozen long stemmed
Red roses delivered at work
Will make her heart skip a
Beat.

A candle light dinner at the

Finest restaurant is
Romantically exquisite.

Sprinkle a basket full of
Lavender rose petals over
The bed and floor prior to
Her entering the room to
Retire for the night, is
Heaven on earth, and
Will never be forgotten.

So Precious

I want to take you out of
The rain, shelter you with
Love, feed and bathe you
With thousands of kisses.
Quench your thirst with
The best champagne;
Clothe you with silk laced
With diamonds and gold.
You are so precious, pure
And worthy, I want to
Offer you the world.

Looking for Love

Since the Creator brought
You to me I talk of love
And radiate like it. I hold
My head high and waltz
Around with it's
Quintessence.

My heart beats with the
Smooth suave fragrance
Of our love, and my pulse
Propels it explicitly. My
Mind sings with its'
Magnificence and my
Lungs exhale it. My skin
Glows from its strength
And my eyes emit rays
Saturated with its spirit.
When I think of you my
Upward facial lines vividly
Displays and expresses the
Adoration I have for you.

I had been looking for love
And now I have it. To play
With, enjoy, work and sleep...

I am truly grateful to God
For spending His precious
Time to produce you for me
And for your miraculous
Beauty, concern, character,
Charm, sophistication and
Unlimited Love. You are
Truly the fruit of my many
Prayers and the love of my
Life.

The Greatness of Our Love

I remember the
North Star, even
The Big Dipper,
The moon was
Settled and bright
As we walked
Holding hands in
The night.

The vapors of the
Air were filled
With love. Every
Step we made
Brought our love,
Closer and more
Sententious,
Crickets were
Present and silent
As well as frogs.

Only the Night
Hawks danced
And chirped
Around in the air.
The bugs were

Rejoicing by
Giving extra
Flashes of light.
The silent night
Was bright
The moon, stars
And even the
Asteroids were
Celebrating one
Of the wonders
Of the world,
The greatness of
Our love.

The Night You Touched My Soul

I've heard of you and I have been
Waiting for you. I have not seen
You, but I know you. I have
Dreamed of you and adore you.
I have truly needed you. I thank
My Lord for you. He has always
Made a way for me, when I needed
Direction and a light to see.

Before my first real contact with
You that lovely silent night. I was
Greatly concerned as to how you
Would be; wondrous, strange, odd,
Receptive or perhaps eccentric?
The hesitation and preoccupation
Of your voice only further perplexed
Me; I waited on time to see. The
Minutes and hours continued and
Out of the dark a bright brilliant
Sunny divine aura came over me.
The longer we spoke the more I
Could see we've been with each
Other before. We have traveled
Many of the same roads, stayed
Many of the same places, done

A lot of the same things. We
Have so much in common what
A delight, to speak and be near
Someone as attractive as you.

A true believer in Christ,
Compassionate, concerned,
True to spirit, mother wit a
Worker for God's people,
Black, proud and more beautiful
Than words. I've been waiting
For you. Lord God sets us free
To do His work; I must and you
Must. Perhaps with time we'll
See if we can serve and work
For Him as one. You are truly a
Glorious person, righteous and
Truthful no end. Until the end
I'll remember that miraculous
Night, "the night you touched
My soul."

V

Natural
Love

Love You and Birds

You are as Proud as a peacock
Parading around to attract a
Lovely peahen. Delicate as a
Hummingbird Colorful as a
Northern cardinal and as
Beautiful as a crown crane.
Your love is more Powerful
Then a giant eagle and as
Determined as a hawk with
A handsome meal in sight.
You are as Wise as an owl,
Striking as a puffin or even
African roller and as Unique
As a flamingo posing on the
Edge of a cliff.

Natural

Sweetheart, you are distinctive
And as natural as the whistling
Wind on a cold lonely night.
The mountains of snow
Sparkling in the dark and the
Enlightening full moon high
In the sky. As the welcome
Bright sun after numerous
Rainy vacation days. The dark
Winter and the wet spring.
The brilliant summer sun and
The changing colors of fall are
As natural as you and my love
For you.

My Flower

The look, and display
Of magnificent beauty
Stunning fragrance with
Unyielding charm.
Pleasing to the eye
Small, but large in life
Lovely and refined
Warm and colorfully
Filled with an abundance
Of peace, joy, grace
And amazing love.

A Single Rose

A single rose connotes
Different intendments.
All associated with
Love joy and
Contentment.

It is an expression of
The beauty of you and
The deep love and trust
That we share and
Embrace.

This precious flower
Binds us to that
Glorious heavenly
State, "the essence of
Life," true love.

Therefore, I offer you
This rose and all the
Love that it stands for
And more.

The African Beach

I see you now with bright
Cloths and sun blessed
Nubian skin, walking
Through the sand.

The palm trees swaying
Back and forth, saluting
And waving as you pass
By.

The ocean breeze is
Refreshing and prominent
Delivering the marine
Fragrance throughout the
Air.

I see the fine mist created
From the continuous waves
Pouncing on the great rocks
Causing miniature droplets
To dance in the air, almost
Swinging into your lovely
Hair.

The colorful sailboats are
Parading across the waters
And others so distant that
They can hardly be seen.
What a lovely scene.

Love Through All the Seasons

I love you through all the
Seasons for thousands of
Reasons. If anyone inquires
About love, I tell them about
You.
Each time I open my eyes
Take a morsel of food, take
A deep breath and exhale,
Move my limbs, see palm
Trees sway in the wind from
The gentle force of a cool
Summer breeze, see colorful
Leaves drift from shedding
Branches of wondrous oak
Trees, marvel at the geometric
Designs of snowflakes, sniff
The essence of spring flowers,
Hear birds sing, see the sunrise
And moon exudes its presence.
It defines love and reminds
Me of how much of it, I have
For you.

Quiet Storm

You came into my life with
All of your charm. Your
Exquisite touch, and elegance
Was beyond imagination. Just
One look is all it took and
I knew the spirit of peace,
Love and tranquility except for
The pine cones crashing down
From distant trees. I could see
The spirit I felt the calm and the
Mighty forces of the wind but
No disturbance and no pain. I
Saw the thunder and lightning
Like effects but no damage was
Done and no rain. I felt the power
And the wonderful spirit a million
Bolts but no pain. A quiet storm.
It was love peaceful and strong.
Just one look, one moment that
Will last beyond our lifetimes.

Flowers for My Lady

I've got flowers for you of all
Types; I will shower you with
Them.

I have gardenias and plumeria
For your lovely hair; and
Tulips for your eyes.

I have rubrium lilies for your
Nose, orchids for you
Stupendous lips.

I have paper whites for your
Great heart, protea for your
Skin.

I have camellias for your
Kindness, daisies for our
Friendship.

I have jasmine for the fragrance
You present, pansies for your
Strength.

I have passion flowers for your
Spirit, red roses for our love.

I have bunches and bunches of
Flowers, my lady and they are
All for you.

Great Wonders

I've seen the oceans sailed
Across many of the seas;
Your love is more wonderful
Than all of these.

I've seen Alaskan glaciers,
Salt Lake, Grand Canyon,
Masai Mara, Serengeti, most
Of the major cities of the
World; your love is more
Exciting than all of these.

I've visited the Pyramids,
Sphinx, Hoover Dam, Eiffel
Tower; Liberty Statue, the
Empire State Building; your
Love is more immense then
All of these.

I've climbed many mountains,
Everest, Kilimanjaro, Kenya,
Godwin Austen, Ruwenzori,
Rainier and McKinley; none
As gigantic or as impressive
As your love.

I've known rivers, the
Amazon, Rhine, Niger,
Mississippi, Nile, Rio
Colorado and Niagara;
None as great as the
Love that flows from
The chambers of your
Heart.

VI

Love You

Sophisticated Lady

Be as elegant as you were made,
Don't change. You were made
Supreme, stand tall you are divine,
Walk your walk, each step like a
Work of art, shoulders back, stand
Tall, you are a gem, shades of black
Minimal to jet, your waist hip ratio
There is no better. You are a true
Queen. There is no beauty beyond
You. Gifted with both physical and
Spiritual beauty. Your glamorous hair
Is a crown declaring your royalty and
Sincerity.
Common, skimpy wear displaying
Your temple is not appealing, the
Same as is gifted black with blond
Hair, which generally looks like____,
Depicting women of the street. Be
Yourself, the Queen, sophisticated
Lady, don't change, the beauty of you.

Just Look

I've got fine clothes but my
Clothes don't make me. I
Make them...look good,
Don't you understand?

Look at my posture, my
Figure and my hips, check
Out the grace; look at the
Walk, see the connection
In the action. The power,
The grace, the strength,
The rhythm, the lift; isn't
It grand?

Look at my ebony skin my
Gifted, lips and my gorgeous
Wool like hair; it's divine,
I'm fine. Just look, don't
Touch.

Let me keep on walking so
You can see how great, I
Make these clothes look.

Take a second look or may
Be three, it's free; if you
Want to take a picture you'll
Have to ask me.

Lessons for Life

Listen to the music of life
And try to do what is right.
Raise your children with
The bible and a firm hand.

Teach your children that
The world that is against
Them still has to answer
To a higher power.

When they have a problem
With the world. They can
Always get help by going
To the source of all power.

They are God's children
And He didn't make a
Mistake. He created them
For a reason. He gave them
Gifts and He loves them no
Matter the color, size or
Shape.

Teach your children to
Respect, honor, obey and

Love your man. In doing
Such the love extends
Beyond generations.

Teach them to pray,
Exercise, read and study
Daily. For it keeps them
Mentally and physically fit,
Healthy, alert,
Knowledgeable, strong
And wise.

Don't let poison such as
Cigarettes enter your
System or let others enter
It into theirs around your
Children.

Feed your children good
Home cooked low fat and
Low carbohydrate meals,
Cut back on fast high
Fat and cholesterol foods.
Don't let your life run around

The soaps and don't let the
Soaps wash away your life
With programmed
Idiosyncratic, codswallop.

Hold, hug and love your
Baby enough to give them
The milk of life from your
Breasts instead of that of
The life of some
Environmentally challenged
Animals. Listen to the spirit
And let it's love lead you to
The sweet music of joy,
Happiness and success.

The Lady of My Dreams

You are the lady
Of my dreams.
Waiting for you
Has taught me how
To handle pain.

I have searched
And toiled, played
And played with.
Spent time, paid
A wealth of dues.
Restless nights,
Until I saw you
Again today, after
Dreaming of you
Many times and
Many nights.

My love,
My angel, my
Sweetheart, my
Queen you are
Everything and
More than what
I need. The lady
Of my dreams.

I See You

Africa, the land of Timbuktu,
Garden of Eden, pyramids,
Jesus, diamonds and gold.

I see you, Black woman,
Proud, colorful, beautiful
And wonderful.

I see your thick coiled
Powerful wool like hair,
Providing protection from
Sun and harsh elements of
The air.

I see your Cleopatra like
Eyes as if they were laced
With belladonna.

I see your gifted nose,
Glamorous complete lips;
Your smooth ebony skin
Cannot be missed.

Your royal figure with
Appropriate top, minimal
Waist and full hips are
The essence of femininity.

You are viewed with
Exception due to your
Unique balance, grace and
Strength.

I see you, Black woman, as
You walk with rhythm to the
Music of life, I see you.

Beautiful You

Beautiful is your name, for after God
Made the sand and the seas, the moon
And the sun the darkness and the light,
Heaven and earth and just before He
Rested on the 7th day. He decided to
Create an image, a very gratifying image
And He had you in mind. He sat and He
Thought about a divine description of an
Appearance that would make the eyes
See what the mind would visualize and
Transmit to our other senses to make us
Respond to this very pleasant image
With delight. He called this likeness, you
And named you and stated that when
Anyone looked at you they to would call
You by your name, Beautiful. Thus, God
Had you in mind and stated that when
Anyone else had your characteristics,
They too would be called beautiful like
You. He had you in mind and He named
Beauty after you, for this was good.

It should be understood that no matter
Where you go. How long you stay, who
You are with or how long you are

Physically around, you were the first to
Be called beautiful.

When the Creator made you, He decided
That the look that you were given would
Represent a distinctive image that would
Be the standard for the pleasing state that
You display. So He named beautiful after
You. That is why the spirit of you is
Joyous, your soul is refined and why your
Smile lights up a room and elevates every
Righteous one there.

It is pleasing to note that the aura of you is
Attached to your magnificent smile, this is
Good, for beauty is in this, and is named
After you.

A Fool in Love

I used to think that I was a fool
In love with you, now I know it
Was foolish. Time and time
Again, I begged and pleaded
For you to do what you know
You should do, that was
Right.
All of my strength and resources
Were devoted to you. That wasn't
Gratifying, you played and teased.
I was looking for love, lonely knew
Of your trials and awful past, felt
Compassion and endless sympathy.
Foolish thoughts, prevailed that our
Foundation was as solid as a rock
Instead it was quicksand.
Thank God, for the strength and
Wisdom obtained from the many
Painful nights of worry and
Concern. I gave you my all.
No regrets, I was in love. It was
Better to have the experience
For a short while and find out

Your true ways than to have
Stayed and lived in misery for
The rest of my days.

A Great Gift to Heal Our Nation

At last, change has come. The 44th President
Of the United States is tall, powerful, physically
Fit, handsome, charismatic, calm, peaceful,
Loving, exact, confident, gifted and black.
With lovely wife and two beautiful children.
He is all of that and the fruit of the victims of
Slave ships. Those from the banks of Europe,
Africa, Asia and beyond. He is that of the
Struggle for righteousness for all people. He
Is that of the many saints such as Tubman,
Douglas, Parks, Martin, Malcolm; the victims
Of segregation, racism, and apartheid.

President Obama and his family will enter
The White House, which was built by slaves.
Their spirit prevails agonized by the suffering,
Trials and tribulations, lack of compensation
Save for perhaps a whip on their back. You can
See them smiling now, appreciating this was
Worth the torture. The spirit of their love is
There to welcome he and his family.

The President electrifies crowds and is the
Hope and faith in a system that for countless
Years appears to deny many of its children
The rights that should have been available to

All. He is that of a little known man a few years
Ago. Who was exponentially moved a head to
The top of world. Inspired by the Almighty and
Destined for victory. Through the struggles of
The many day and nights of the campaign to
Win an election that was won before it began.
It was in God's hands and it could only have
Been of His desire and ordination. When it
Was won people in America of all types and
Throughout the world was rejoicing beyond
Belief. The station of the United States is that
We are what we say we are and that they now
Truly know that very fact.

Millions bound as one by the magnitude of our
Creator's love, viewed the inexplicable inauguration.
Angels diligently cooled the billows of energized air
Providing comfort from the extreme warmth formed
By the wealth of happiness and joy. In the presence of
The icy temperature in Washington, D.C.
It is gratifying
To see such a man as this that God has chosen to be the
Leader of the most powerful nation in the world, to
Help lift us up from the pit that we are now in. We are
One, one nation, one people under one loving God
Regardless of the position, color, culture or race and
One great chosen leader, Barack Obama.

Queen of the Universe

God made the Black female very
Special. She is the mother and the
Queen of the universe; everyone
Came from her. She has stood the
Test of time, enduring hardship,
Suffering, trials and tribulations.

She has survived the slave castles
And ships, tortures, rapes and
Genocide. She has witnessed the
Murdering of husband and son.
She has been raped by evil
Oppressive slave owners and
Forced to watch while he sold
Their own children!

The Black woman has worked
Hard all day, nurse hers' and
The slave owner's all night.
She has been treated like trash
Worse than animals, can you
Imagine? She has been whipped
And sold, separated from family
And friends.

Today she is still enduring the
Battle and fighting the war. Her
Children, especially the male
Ones, are being drugged,
Wrongfully jailed and slaughtered
Everyday. She is being challenged
More than ever by evil isms, racism
Satanism, klanism, joblessness and
Family torn at both ends. Her
Communities flooded with guns,
Drugs, daily killings and crime to
The highest degree.

She will win the battle and the war,
For God is on her side. God has made
Her special, that's why in spite of it
All she has stood proud and strong,
Fighting every evil move that is
Made. What other woman could have
Endured so much but still remain
Sane? "Yes," only the Queen. The
Black female, thank God for her.
For without her, there would
Be no you or I.

VII

Eternal
Love

Beyond Eternity

As I look up at the
Sky and view the
Cluster of cotton
Like clouds. I am
Thankful to God
For giving us love.

Love was present
Before I physically
Met you before we
Were born before
Mountains were
Formed before the
Seas were made,
Before stars were
Made to shine,
Before night and
Day before the sun
Projected its rays.

Love was there
Before rivers were
Made to flow and
Ice bergs and
Glaciers were ever

Heard of, before the
Mighty sun was able
To beam its rays
Through the skies on
Our land before there
Was the wind, clouds
Or storms before there
Was a north or south,
East or west? It was
There.

Our love was there
God thought it and
Made it. Before He
Made a grain of sand
Even before the Garden
Of Eden, our love was
There, then now and
Beyond eternity.

Life

Life is sometimes funny and
Sometimes strange. For some
People, life is a fantasy like
World; not thinking that there
Are strains and pains, ups and
Downs, rainy and sunny days,
Joy and sorrow, tears and
Smiles, lemon and honey.
They think life is a bowl of
Cherries, without the seeds.
Sweetheart, I have the bowl
I will turn fantasy into reality.
Here are the cherries without
Seeds and I will provide what
Ever else you desire for the
Rest of our days.

Love Will Never Let Us Part

As I travel further and
Further away, it must
Be stated that our love
Gets closer and closer.
I see you now as we
Parted. I held you close
And our embrace is still
Vivid as if it is still present.
I can savor your fragrance
I can feel your lips I see
Your brown eyes even your
Red dress.

I remember the day before
As we walked through the
Rose garden holding hands
And drinking champagne;
Even last night under the
Stars the moon filled the
Night and the fragrance,
The spirit of you made the
Crickets excited and the
Camouflaged frogs to make
Their love call.

The seat beside me may be
Empty but my heart and
Mind is saturated with you.
I can even smell your
Perfume, and it won't be
Long until I see you again
But until then, remember,
Love will never ever let
Us part.

A Special Moment

I had a problem with
Love, God solved it in
A moment by bringing
You me. I am more than
Pleased for this.

My heart dances and
Shouts when I think about
You and the special moment
We first met. As I stand here
Viewing the sky, the stars
The prominent moon and the
Peacefulness of the night.
The peace of this moment
Takes me back in time. When
It was just you, God and I,
Divine, refined, heavenly,
More.

Love, the moment we met
A precious moment like no
Other. The essence of which
Could never be misplaced

Destroyed, forgotten or
Abolished. One moment of
Love that will last more than
Forever.

Your Love

Your love is the sunshine that
Lights up the day. It is the glow
Of the moon at it's greatest
Diameter at midnight. It is the
Force that makes my heart race
When I see your beatific smile.
It has the power of a hurricane
And the peace of a silent winter
Night. It is treacly, even sweeter
Than a mountain of stevia, mixed
With the essence of the substance
From precious hives. It is Longer
Than time, beyond space and
Unlimited size. My love is yours
And yours is mine for the end of time.

God is on Your Side

The resultant of two of the most
Precious people known, a match
Par excellent. God put them
Together. He gentle, stalwart,
Kind, a picture of strength with a
Gargantuan heart. She full of joy,
Strong, gregarious, loving and a
Smile that is everlasting. Each with
The same elevated miraculous
Spirit of goodness, kindness and
Altruism.

God made your parents distinctive,
Protects them, guides them, you are
Of them, their seed. God will do for
You, as He has done for them. His
Armor is the greatest of protection
And cannot be penetrated by any
Enemy. For these continue your daily
Prayers as will we. Be strong, you are
Great, keep the faith, smile. God is on
Your side, forever and always. Home
Soon, safe, joyous and sound.

1st Lt. Denard Fobbs, Jr., September 2008

My Love for You

Darling, I've often pondered
And wondered about the
Extent of my love for you?
Through time, I've come to
Realize that many things
About my love for you are
True. It's purer than the
Fresh soothing drops of
Spring time rain. It's higher
Than the North Star. It is
Larger than the earth is
Wide and deeper than
Fathoms can describe. It's
More valuable than gold
And as dear to me as my
Soul. It's for eternity
And I love you.

It's All About Love

Dr. Leonard Weather is available
for speaking engagements...

To Render:

♥ *Inspirational Presentations*

♥ *Cultural Presentations*

♥ *Spiritual Presentations*

♥ *Motivational Presentations*

♥ *Health and Wellness Presentations*

Leonard Weather Jr., M.D.
2120 Bert Kouns Loop
Suite C
Shreveport, LA 71118

Phone: (318) 671-5320

Email: dr_weather@msn.com or
dr_weather@bellsouth.net

Website: www.drweather.com